Eeyore's Gloomy Little
Instruction Book

Look out for these other not-so-gloomy
Little titles from Methuen

Available from all good bookshops

EEYORE'S gloomy LITTLE INSTRUCTION BOOK

INSPIRED BY *A. A. Milne*

WITH DECORATIONS BY *Ernest H. Shepard*

METHUEN

First published in Great Britain in 1997 by Methuen
an imprint of Reed International Books Limited
Michelin House, 81 Fulham Road, London SW3 6RB
and Auckland, Melbourne, Singapore and Toronto
Published in the United States 1996 by Dutton Children's Books
a division of Penguin Books USA, Inc.
Copyright © 1996 by the Trustees of the Pooh Properties
This presentation © 1996 by Dutton Children's Books
Text by A.A. Milne and illustrations by E.H. Shepard
from *When We Were Very Young, Winnie-the-Pooh, Now We Are Six,*
and *The House At Pooh Corner*
Copyright under the Berne Convention
Written by Joan Powers Designed by Adrian Leichter

Printed in China

ISBN 0 416 19420 6

1 3 5 7 9 10 8 6 4 2

Remember, nobody minds,
nobody cares.

———◆———

When someone says "How-do-you-do,"
just say that you didn't.

*Just when you think no one
has taken any notice of your birthday,
here come two friends with an empty
honey pot and a broken balloon.*

Don't apologize for merriment and what-not. It's just what would *happen.*

—◄●►—

Do join in the search for a lost friend-or-relation. But don't be surprised when nobody bothers to tell you he's been found, and you search on alone for two days.

When stuck in the river, it is best to dive and swim to the bank yourself before someone drops a large stone on your chest in an attempt to hoosh *you there.*

When your house has quite disappeared, you mustn't complain. You still have all that snow to do with what you like.

"They're funny things,
Accidents. You never have them
till you're having them."

—Eeyore, *The House At Pooh Corner*

Just because you hear a buzzing-noise coming from a tree doesn't mean you're going to get any honey.

"No Give and Take. No Exchange of Thought. It gets you nowhere, particularly if the other person's tail is only just in sight for the second half of the conversation."

—Eeyore, *The House At Pooh Corner*

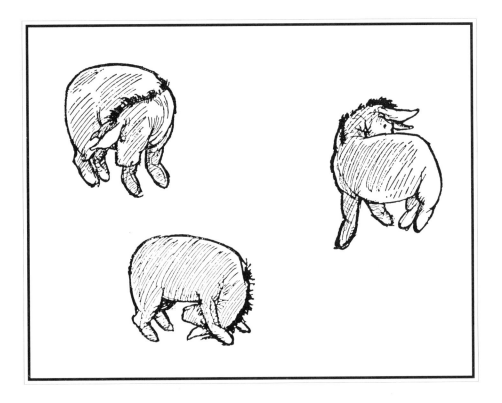

*If it seems as though you haven't
"felt at all how" for a long time, look behind you.
It could be that your tail is missing.*

———◆◆———

*When your tail is missing, remember
that you have every right to Mope.*

*Having your missing tail recovered is
all well and good, but remember that it will have
to be reattached. With a hammer and nail.*

"Pooh is a real friend. Not like Some."

—Eeyore, *The House At Pooh Corner*

If you get yourself stuck in someone's doorway (because you ate too much in the first place), you'll have to let your host use your back legs as a towel-horse. That's just the way it is.

"It isn't as if there was anything very wonderful about my little corner. Of course for people who like cold, wet, ugly bits it *is* something rather special."

—Eeyore, *The House At Pooh Corner*

There are those who will wish you a good morning. If it is a good morning, which is doubtful.

It's bad enough being miserable, but it is even worse when everyone else claims to be miserable, too.

*Anybody who tells you that getting
thin takes "about a week" is lying.*

———◆———

*You never can tell with bees—
or bears, piglets, rabbits, owls…*

Sing. Enjoy yourself. Some can.

"We can't all, and some of us don't.
That's all there is to it."

—Eeyore, *Winnie-the-Pooh*

"You don't always
want to be miserable on
my birthday, do you?"

—Eeyore, *Winnie-the-Pooh*

Building yourself a house is a good idea. But don't be surprised if it winds up on the other side of the wood.

It is always preferable to have a private conversation during a Short Walk, not a Jostle.

*Go ahead, eat all you want.
But just try squeezing out the doorway.*

"No brain at all, some of them."

—Eeyore, *The House At Pooh Corner*

*Sitting on thistles doesn't
do them any Good. Takes all the
Life out of them.*

The only thing worse than being last in line on an Expotition is having half a dozen friends-and-relations behind you who have to be brushed away every time you want to sit down for a little rest. When that is the case, the Expotition becomes simply a Confused Noise.

*When attempting a water rescue,
try putting your tail into the water for
the swimmer to catch on to. Of course,
the tail will lose all feeling.*

———————◆◆———————

*It's always nice to hear about a party—
knowing that they'll be sending you down the
odd bits which got trodden on.*

A numbed tail can be brought back with a good bit of rubbing—until it Belongs again.

———◆◆———

If you think rolling in the mud will help you look like a small black cloud, you are wrong. You'll still look like you—only dirtier.

"Nobody tells me.
Nobody keeps me Informed.
I make it seventeen days come
Friday since anybody
spoke to me."

—Eeyore, *The House At Pooh Corner*

*When trying to rescue friends from
a tree, make sure the plan doesn't involve
having everybody stand on your back.*

*U*se caution when standing by the
riverbank, minding your own business.
You might get bounced into the water.

"It will rain soon, you see if it doesn't."

—Eeyore, *Winnie-the-Pooh*

*Don't be discouraged
to discover that A is a thing
Rabbit knows.*

"Everybody crowds round so
in this Forest. There's no Space.
I never saw a more Spreading lot of
animals in my life, and all in
the wrong places."

—Eeyore, *The House At Pooh Corner*

*Even at the very bottom of
the river, don't stop to say to yourself,
"Is this a Hearty Joke, or is it the Merest
Accident?" Just float to the surface
and say to yourself, "It's wet."*

"They haven't got Brains, any of them, only grey fluff that's blown into their heads by mistake, and they don't Think."

—Eeyore, *The House At Pooh Corner*

*Looking for the North Pole
or playing "Here we go gathering Nuts
and May" with the end part of an
ant's nest—it's all the same.*

*N*o self-respecting bee would be fooled
into thinking that a muddy bear holding on to a
balloon was actually a small black cloud—even if
someone was walking below, carrying an umbrella
and saying, "Tut-tut, it looks like rain."

*If, after you've fed a guest, he
looks longingly in the direction of the larder,
it probably means that he wants more
food. Tell him there isn't any.*

"Don't Bustle me. Don't now-then me."

—Eeyore, *The House At Pooh Corner*

Whenever a Very Bouncy Animal arrives in the Forest, and you are told that he has just come, the thing you should ask is: "When is he going?"

Small applause is better than no applause, even when it is a little lacking in Smack.

"I don't hold with
all this washing. This modern
Behind-the-ears nonsense."

—Eeyore, *Winnie-the-Pooh*

*If you don't like thistles,
don't bend a perfectly good one.*

"Bouncy or coffy, it's all the same
at the bottom of the river."

—Eeyore, *The House At Pooh Corner*

"Owl flew past a day or two ago and noticed me. He didn't actually say anything, mind you, but he knew it was me. Very friendly of him, I thought. Encouraging."

—Eeyore, *The House At Pooh Corner*

*K*eep bouncy, stripy animals
away from your favorite thistle patch. One
doesn't want one's lunch bounced on.

"I'm telling you. People come and
go in this Forest, and they say, 'It's only
Eeyore, so it doesn't count.' "

—Eeyore, *The House At Pooh Corner*

*Don't be surprised when
you notice that your house is still standing,
even though it seems as though somebody ought
to have come and knocked it down. Maybe
they figure the wind will do it.*

*Climbing trees in search of
honey is a bad idea. You'll fall.
Probably into a gorse-bush.*

Don't be surprised if it hails a good deal tomorrow. Blizzards and what-not. Being fine today doesn't Mean Anything. It's just a small piece of weather.

"It's snowing still.
And freezing. However, we haven't
had an earthquake lately."

—Eeyore, *The House At Pooh Corner*

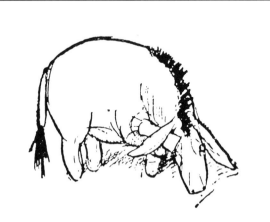

Move about more. Come and go.
And if anybody says in a Loud Voice
"Bother," you can drop out again.

"Don't Blame Me."

—Eeyore, *Winnie-the-Pooh*

*Poohsticks isn't as much fun
as everyone thinks, especially if you are
the one floating under the bridge.*

"A tail isn't a tail
to *them,* it's just a Little Bit Extra
at the back."

—Eeyore, *Winnie-the-Pooh*

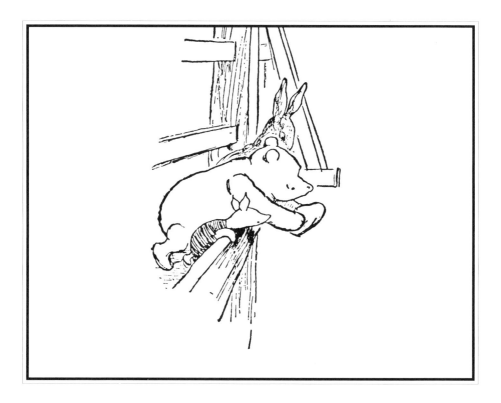

Beware of ideas others come up with for rescuing you from the river, especially if they involve dropping a heavy stone right on you.

When you shout "Is anybody at home?" into a rabbit hole, and a voice answers "No!" it probably means you're not welcome.

"Sometimes, when people have
quite finished taking a person's house,
there are one or two bits which they don't
want and are rather glad for the person to
take back, if you know what I mean."

—Eeyore, *The House At Pooh Corner*

When your tail happens to be missing, someone will try to convince you that you left it somewhere. But you'll know that somebody must have taken it.

"After all, what are
birthdays? Here today
and gone tomorrow."

—Eeyore, *The House At Pooh Corner*

*When Rabbit comes up importantly and says
"Ah, Eeyore," you can be certain he will be saying
"Good-bye" in about two more minutes.*

"What with all this snow, not
to mention icicles and such-like, it isn't
so Hot in my field about three o'clock in the
morning. In fact, quite-between-ourselves-
and-don't-tell-anybody, it's Cold."

—Eeyore, *The House At Pooh Corner*

A little Consideration, a little Thought for Others, makes all the difference. Or so they say.

If you've been invited to a party, it's probably a mistake. Make sure they don't blame you if it rains.

eOR

This writing business—
pencils and what-not—is overrated.
Silly stuff. Nothing in it.

"One can't complain. I have my friends.
Somebody spoke to me only yesterday."

—Eeyore, *Winnie-the-Pooh*